3-90

D0313340

# Coming Home

## BOB READ

Published in association with The Basic Skills Agency

# Hodder & Stoughton

A MEMBER OF THE HODDER HEADLINE GROUP

100952

A CIP record is available from the British Library

ISBN 0340 590343

First published 1993
New edition 1996
Impression number   10  9  8  7  6  5  4
Year                      1999  1998  1997  1996

Printed in Great Britain for Hodder & Stoughton Educational,
a division of Hodder Headline Plc, 338, Euston Road, London NW1 3BH
by Redwood Books, Trowbridge, Wiltshire.

# 1

Cathy looked at the clock on the dashboard. In the darkness of the car the hands and numbers were bright green, like an alarm clock. It was two o'clock in the morning. It would be almost three by the time she got home, she thought.

The road to Denby in front of her was almost dead straight for six miles. It cut straight across the flat Norfolk marshland to the coast. At this time of night there were not many cars on the road. In her headlights a line of bright cat's eyes led off into the darkness. On one side of the road, in the distance, Cathy could see the little white lights of a village, like ships far out on a dark sea.

It was a cold November night. Cathy was driving home after a meeting in London. She worked as a sales rep for a company that sold luggage. The trains had been on strike, and so she had driven down to London early that morning. After the meeting she had been asked out to dinner by her sales manager. That had made her very late leaving London that evening.

Inside the car it was warm. Cathy turned the heater down a little bit. She was beginning to feel sleepy. She opened her window just a little bit to get some air. The cold winter wind rushed in.

It was cold, but at least it was fresh, clean air. Cathy could tell that she was now just a few miles from the sea. In London the air always felt stale. It gave Cathy a headache. She was glad to be out of London and almost home.

The wind was so cold that she was glad to close the window again. It would be awful to break down here, she thought. It was so cold and dark and lonely. She looked up along the line of cat's eyes to the only bend in the long straight road to Denby.

On the bend there was a T-junction. So many accidents had happened there that the whole bend was now lit with a line of orange street lights. After so many miles of winter darkness the lights looked warm and cheerful.

As Cathy slowed down to take the bend, she thought she saw a person standing under one of the lights. It looked like a young woman. She wore jeans and a white blouse. She was waving her arms. Cathy slowed down. She must be in trouble, she thought. I will have to stop.

Cathy pulled up by the side of the road just before she reached the girl. It felt strange to be stopping in the middle of nowhere. She hoped she was doing the right thing.

# 2

Cathy watched the girl as she walked towards the car. The girl looked strange in the orange light from the street lamps. But then everything looks strange under those orange lights, Cathy thought. She had noticed that before in the town. They didn't seem to cast any real shadows.

As the girl walked into the headlights, Cathy could see her clearly. She was in her twenties, with long dark hair. Her face looked very pale. She must be really cold with just a blouse on, Cathy thought. Had she had an accident? But, if so, where was her car?

Cathy was just reaching over to open the window to talk to her, when the girl opened the car door. Cathy felt frightened. She was sure the door had been locked. The girl got into the passenger seat.

'Are you OK? Did you want a lift?' Cathy asked.

'I want to go home,' the girl said softly.

Cathy switched on the little light by the rearview mirror and looked at the girl. The girl was staring down at her hands in her lap. Her long dark hair hid most of her face. Cathy looked at her white blouse and her jeans. She must be freezing, Cathy thought. But what on earth was she doing at two in the

morning by the side of the road? Cathy looked out into the darkness for the girl's car, but she saw nothing.

'Have you had a crash or something?' Cathy asked. The girl did not answer. She lifted her hand to her face. She rubbed her forehead just above her right eye. She seemed to frown, as if she had a headache.

'I want to go home,' she said again softly and looked down into her lap.

There was something wrong with this girl, Cathy thought. She must have had an accident of some sort. Cathy decided she would drive her straight to the hospital at Denby and ask them to ring the police. She turned to reach for a blanket from the back seat. It was a red and blue tartan car rug that her mother had given her as a birthday present. She put it around the shoulders of the girl. She knew that a person in shock had to be kept warm.

Cathy suddenly felt very cold herself too. She put the car in gear. It would soon warm up, she thought. Cathy drove off quickly towards Denby. In the distance, the bottom edge of the dark night sky was coloured orange by the lights of the town. The girl sat in silence beside her.

Cathy noticed the girl rub her forehead again with her hand.

'Do you feel OK?' Cathy asked.

The girl said nothing. She looked straight ahead into the darkness.

'Do you feel a bit warmer now?' Cathy asked.

The girl said nothing.

Cathy herself still felt very cold. She looked down to see if she had turned on the heater. The control was set at red. It should have been full on. That was strange, Cathy thought. Just a few minutes ago it had felt quite warm.

# 3

As Cathy drove into Denby, she came to a roundabout.

'Left here, if you can,' the girl said. 'I live just off the main road on the left.'

Cathy thought for a moment. She had planned to drive straight to the hospital. But the girl seemed sure of where she was going. And anyway, Cathy thought, her parents will be wondering where she is. They will be able to take care of her.

'OK. If you tell me the way, I'll take you home,' Cathy said.

She was glad the girl had said something at last. Perhaps she had felt shocked and frightened when she first got into the car, Cathy thought. Now that the girl was near home she was probably feeling more herself.

The girl asked her to take two more turnings left. It was not a part of the town that Cathy knew well. As she took the second turning left, she saw the name of the road in her headlights. It was Blake Road.

The girl asked Cathy to pull in half-way down the road. Cathy stopped under a street light and could see the number 58 on the gate post.

She put on the handbrake and switched off the engine. The headlights of the car faded quickly. It was dark in the car. The light from the street lamp fell on the girl's hands, which were folded in her lap. Cathy noticed a ring on her right hand. It was a gold signet ring with the letter A.

'I am home now,' the girl said softly. She turned to look at Cathy and smiled. 'Thank you,' she said and began to open the car door.

'No, wait a moment. I'll come with you,' Cathy began to say as the girl got out of the car.

Cathy wanted to go with the girl up to the house, so that she could explain to her family how she had found the girl out on the road to Denby. She got out of the car to follow the girl. As she shut the door, she looked across the roof of the car. There was no one there.

She walked round on to the pavement and looked up the drive to the house. She looked down the road. The street lights gleamed on the roofs of a line of parked cars, but the girl was nowhere to be seen. Cathy stood still and listened for the sound of footsteps. She could hear nothing. Just the ticking of her car engine as it cooled.

Suddenly Cathy felt very frightened. It was very late at night, and she was alone in a street she did not know. That girl had seemed strange right from the start, she thought. And now she had vanished. Cathy ran back to the car. The click of her heels on the empty road made her feel even more alone.

She got into the car and switched on the engine. She felt frightened. Picking up the girl seemed like a strange dream now. She wanted to get back home quickly. As she pulled away, she could feel that the air coming out of the vents by her feet was very warm. At the road junction she stopped to turn the heater down a little. That's strange, she thought. The heater was working normally now.

As she looked down at the dashboard to adjust the heater control, she caught sight of the clock on the dashboard. She could not believe what she saw. The bright green hands on the clock face were still pointing to two o'clock.

=================================

# 4

The next day Cathy was late up, but it did not really matter. She had to prepare for a sales meeting in Norwich, but that was not till two in the afternoon. Her husband, Dave, had already left for work, so she felt she could take her time over breakfast.

Cathy turned on the radio and began to fill the kettle for some tea. She felt in a good mood. She enjoyed being on her own at the start of the day. It was like being single again, she thought.

On the window-sill she saw a flask and a box of sandwiches. Dave had forgotten to take them to work. She turned the tap off and stopped to think for a moment. The flask had reminded her of something. It was something she herself had forgotten. On the radio she could hear a breakfast DJ talking and laughing. His chatter made it hard for her to think clearly. Still, it would come back to her, she thought.

She went to fetch the milk. As she opened the front door, the cold air made her catch her breath. The winter sunshine was bright, but there was still frost on the grass and on the car windows. She bent down to pick up the milk. The glass of the bottles felt cool between her fingers. It had been very cold last night, she thought.

She had woken Dave up when she had got home and told him all about the strange girl. She felt he had not believed her when she had told him about the heater and the clock.

Cathy took the milk back into the kitchen and made the tea. When her toast was ready, she sat down at the breakfast table with the morning newspaper. The table stood in a wide warm track of sunshine that came in through the kitchen window. Cathy felt relaxed and happy. Perhaps she did not have such a bad life as a sales rep, she thought. She had to drive a lot on her own, but then there were mornings like this when she had time to herself.

She picked up a knife and looked behind the newspaper for the jam and the marmalade. In the bright sunshine that fell across the table the jar of marmalade seemed filled with a golden light. It cast an orange shadow on the white tablecloth. Cathy began to think again of the orange street lights on the bend where she had picked up the girl. Even last night it had all seemed strange. Now it seemed even more like a dream. For a moment she looked out of the window, lost in thought.

Her eyes focused on the flask and sandwiches on the window-sill. Suddenly she remembered what it was she had forgotten. The tartan pattern on the flask had reminded her of the rug she had given the girl last night. The girl had walked off with the rug still around her shoulders, and Cathy hadn't had a chance to ask for it back.

I will have to try to find the girl and ask for the rug back, Cathy thought. It had been a present from her mother. And anyway she wanted to find out how the girl was. Cathy looked at her watch. It was 10.45. She still had two or three hours before her meeting in Norwich. She remembered the address: 58 Blake Road.

She quickly cleared the table and left the washing-up in the sink. She picked up her car keys and went out to the car in such a rush that she forgot to turn the radio off. As she pulled away, the DJ chattered on and on to himself in the kitchen, mad and cheerful and lonely, like a caged bird.

# 5

Cathy parked on Blake Road outside number 58.
As she got out of the car, she looked down the road
and thought back to the night before.

In the bright sunshine the road seemed very
different. All the cars had gone. A line of small trees
ran along the side of the road. The bare branches
looked clear and sharp against the pale blue
November sky. The gutters were full of fallen
leaves, and in the cold sharp air there was the smell
of wood smoke. From a bonfire somewhere,
Cathy thought.

A lady walked by with a dog and said hello.
It seemed a quiet, friendly road. Cathy could not
believe how frightened she had felt in the same road
the night before.

She undid the latch on the gate post.

The garden path was thick with fallen leaves.
They crackled under her feet as she walked up the
path. She did not know what she was going to say
when she called at the house. It was such a strange
story. She felt nervous as she rang the doorbell.

There was no answer. In a way, Cathy was relieved.
Perhaps she should just forget about last night and
about the girl.

But as she turned to walk back down the path, she still felt a little disappointed. Something in Cathy that made her a good sales rep did not want to give up that easily. She stopped walking to look at her watch. She needed to think for a moment.

The sound of dry leaves being brushed and crushed by her feet also stopped. As it became quiet, Cathy could hear a strange clicking noise. It seemed to come from the back garden.

She went back and followed the path around the side of the house. In the back garden by a greenhouse she saw a woman with grey hair standing by a long row of tall yellow flowers. She was cutting them with a small pair of pruning shears.

'Good morning,' Cathy called out to the woman.

The sound of Cathy's voice made the woman jump. She turned around quickly to see who it was.

'Hello,' the woman said when she saw Cathy.

Cathy could see the woman looked worried. In a rush, she began to explain, 'I'm sorry I made you jump. I did ring at the front door, but there was no answer. My name is Cathy Bell. I think it was perhaps your daughter I met late last night. A young girl about twenty with long dark hair. I gave her a lift home, you see.'

The woman put her hand to her mouth. She looked shocked by what Cathy had said.

Cathy felt worried too. She had not been expecting the woman to react in this way.

'Is she all right?' Cathy asked.

'Do you mean my daughter Ann?' the woman asked.

Cathy thought quickly. She remembered she had seen the letter A on the girl's ring.

'Yes, I think so. This *is* number 58, isn't it?' Cathy asked.

'Yes. It is. This is Ann's home,' the woman said. Her face had gone very pale.

'But she died a month ago.'

———————

# 6

For several moments Cathy could not move or say anything. She watched the woman bend down to pick up the basket full of yellow flowers. When she stood up, she said to Cathy, 'I knew something must have happened last night. Let's go indoors and talk.'

Cathy followed the woman back to the house and into the kitchen. She felt dazed and shocked.

'I'll just put these flowers in the sink for the moment,' the lady said. Cathy stood and watched the woman as she ran some water into the sink. The sound of the water drumming on the bottom of the aluminium sink seemed to wake Cathy up from her daze.

'I'm terribly sorry, Mrs ... ' Cathy began to say.

'It's Mrs Brooks. But please call me Molly. Let's go into the living room. We'll be more comfortable there.'

As they walked into the living room, Cathy saw a photograph next to a clock on the mantelpiece. It was a photograph of the girl she had met last night. She was riding a horse across an open field. She was smiling and waving her hand at the person taking the picture.

'That's Ann, isn't it?' Cathy asked. The girl was wearing a riding hat, but Cathy recognised her smile. It was the same smile the girl had given her last night, as she got out of the car.

'Yes. It was taken a week before the accident.'

'Was it a car accident?' Cathy asked.

'Yes. It happened on the long straight road into Denby from Norwich,' Mrs Brooks began to explain.

Mrs Brooks sat down in an armchair. Cathy walked over to the mantelpiece to take a closer look at the photograph. Yes, it was definitely the girl she had met last night.

'Was it on that bend near the T-junction?' Cathy asked.

'Yes. A car just pulled out in front of her. It was one of those really foggy nights in early autumn. You know how bad it can be on that road with the fog coming in off the marshes,' Mrs Brooks said.

Cathy turned to look at her. She already knew the answer to the next question, but she had to find out for sure.

'What time did it happen?' Cathy asked.

'It happened at two o'clock in the morning. Ann was on her way home from visiting a friend in Norwich,' Mrs Brooks said. 'But something happened last night, didn't it? You said you thought you had met Ann. What happened?'

Cathy sat down on a settee next to Mrs Brooks. She told her the strange story about how she had met the girl the night before. Mrs Brooks sat quietly, with her hands folded in her lap. She listened carefully as Cathy talked. Several times she nodded.

When Cathy had finished talking, Mrs Brooks said nothing for a moment. She looked down at her hands. She seemed very deep in thought. Then she looked up at Cathy.

'I knew something had happened last night. You see, Ann died of head injuries, and ever since the accident I have had this bad headache, just here.' She rubbed her forehead just above her right eye.

'The doctor said it was just the shock and gave me some tablets to help me sleep. But they didn't help. They never do, do they? I would sleep for an hour, then wake up, and the headache would still be there. I just couldn't settle. I felt worried and on edge all the time, like when you wait up late for someone. You just can't rest till you know they're home again.

'Several people said it was the shock,' Mrs Brooks went on. 'They said it was all part of adjusting to Ann not being here. Last night was just like all the others. I woke up just after one o'clock with the same headache and decided to get up for a while.

'I was sitting here in this room when I felt my headache begin to lift. As my head cleared, I began to feel very, very tired and I went to bed. I slept till late this morning.' Mrs Brooks smiled and went on,

'It was the first good night's sleep I have had for a whole month.'

'What time was it when you felt your headache begin to lift?' Cathy asked.

'It was about two o'clock.'

===============================

# 7

Cathy felt shocked and confused. She stood up and walked to the window. She wanted to think over what Mrs Brooks had told her.

She looked out of the window at the garden in the November sunshine. After talking so much about the strange events of the night before, everything in the world outside looked clear and bright and real. The blue sky. The dark bare branches of the trees. The yellow and brown leaves that lay all over the lawn and the path. Everything looked so real, Cathy thought. But what about last night? Was all of that real too? she asked herself.

A sudden gust of wind lifted some of the dry leaves into the air. They spun and chased each other across the driveway. Like my thoughts, going round and round in circles, Cathy said to herself.

She turned back to look at Mrs Brooks.

'What does it all mean?' Cathy asked.

'I don't think I can even begin to explain it,' Mrs Brooks said. 'But I just keep thinking of how I have felt the last four weeks and how I feel now. A part of me knows that in a way Ann has come home now.'

The clock on the mantelpiece chimed.
Cathy remembered her meeting in Norwich and looked at her watch.

'I'm afraid I shall have to be going,' Cathy said.

'Yes. Of course. I shall have to make a move as well,' Mrs Brooks said.

'Can I offer you a lift anywhere?' Cathy asked.

'Well, yes, if you don't mind. With the accident and everything we don't have a car at the moment.
I was going to take those flowers from the garden down to the cemetery.'

Cathy waited while Mrs Brooks wrapped the bunch of yellow flowers in newspaper. She began to think more and more about the sales meeting in Norwich. *That* was something real. She would have to give a report about her trip to London and she had not prepared anything.

They would want her to talk about sales targets and new products. She tried to think of a way out of giving the report. They would think her mad if she told them she had spent the morning finding out about this strange girl.

Perhaps it helped Mrs Brooks to think that this whole story meant something, Cathy thought.
But, for her part, she decided to put it to the back of her mind. It was a strange story, but nothing more than that.

# 8

As they drove to the cemetery, Cathy talked about her job and her car, about her husband and the weather. She felt she wanted to talk about anything except what had happened the night before. She had felt strange and nervous all morning, ever since she had met Mrs Brooks. She needed to relax a little and feel normal again before she went to the meeting in Norwich.

At the cemetery, Cathy drove in slowly through the wide iron gates. It seemed very quiet after the noise of the traffic in the town. Mrs Brooks asked her to follow the gravel drive around to the far side. They drove quietly past rows of tall pine trees.

Mrs Brooks asked Cathy to stop by a bench. Near the bench was a tap and several grey watering cans. As she got out of the car, Mrs Brooks thanked Cathy for the lift.

'That's OK. I'm only sorry I can't stay to give you a lift back, but I must really be getting off now to my meeting,' Cathy said.

'You must call by and see me again when you have more time, Cathy,' Mrs Brooks said.

Cathy thanked her for the invitation and waved goodbye. As she started the car again, she looked at her watch.

It was 1.15. All at once she began to think quickly about the best way to drive to Norwich, where she would park, and what she would say at the meeting.

There were no other cars in the cemetery, but out of habit Cathy went to look over her shoulder before pulling away. The car was barely moving, but the shock of what she saw made her brake sharply in the gravel. The car stalled. Her hands began to shake as she reached to take out the key from the ignition. She knew she would not be going to the meeting that afternoon.

Cathy had seen Mrs Brooks walking towards a grave. On the corner of the white gravestone hung a red and blue tartan car rug.

═══════════